Yellowstone

Our First National Park

Jane Pecorella

Rosen Classroom Books & Materials
New York

Published in 2003 by The Rosen Publishing Group, Inc.
29 East 21st Street, New York, NY 10010

Book Design: Haley Wilson

Photo Credits: Cover, p. 1 © Gary Randall/FPG International; pp. 4, 12–13 © Josef Beck/FPG International; p. 7 © Kent Miles/FPG International; pp. 9, 11 (President Grant) © Corbis; p. 11 © L. Clarke/Corbis; p. 15 © Thomas Del Brase © Stone; pp. 16–17, 17 (bighorn sheep) © Joseph Van Os/Image Bank; p. 17 (elk) © Steve Hix/FPG International; p. 19 © Paul McCormick/Image Bank; pp. 20–21 © Ted Wood/Stone.

ISBN: 0-8239-6401-9
6-pack ISBN: 0-8239-9590-9

Manufactured in the United States of America

Contents

MONTANA

NORTH DAKOTA

IDAHO

YELLOWSTONE

SOUTH DAKOTA

WYOMING

NEBRASKA

UTAH

COLORADO

Yellowstone National Park

Yellowstone National Park is one of the most beautiful wildlife parks in the United States. It is also one of our largest national parks, with over 2 million acres of land. That is larger than some states!

Most of Yellowstone is in the northwest corner of Wyoming, but some parts are in Idaho and Montana. The park was named Yellowstone because of a type of yellow rock that is found near the park.

Most of Yellowstone is covered by forests. Mountains surround the park on three sides. Yellowstone also has high waterfalls!

Natural Beauty

Yellowstone is known for its natural beauty. Mountains called the Teton Range rise up into the sky. Rushing rivers cut through deep **canyons** (KAN-yunz). Wild animals wander freely through the park.

Thousands of years ago, **volcanoes** and **glaciers** (GLAY-shurz) helped shape the land. Most of the Yellowstone we see today was created over 600,000 years ago when a huge volcano **erupted** and changed the land forever.

Yellowstone is one of the last large wilderness areas remaining in the United States. Many kinds of birds and animals live in its forests, meadows, lakes, and rivers.

Early Visitors

Native Americans had already lived and hunted in Yellowstone for many years before anyone else arrived. A **trapper** named John Colter was probably the first **pioneer** to see Yellowstone. In about 1807, he hiked through the area by himself. More trappers, traders, and hunters soon came to Yellowstone. They told other people about the things they had seen there. Soon, more and more visitors traveled to Yellowstone to see it for themselves.

Some of the first visitors to Yellowstone were men who were searching for animal skins for trading.

The First National Park

Around 1870, the United States Congress sent a team of men to **explore** Yellowstone country. An artist and a photographer went with them. They brought back photographs and paintings of Yellowstone. When members of Congress saw the beautiful pictures, they decided to **protect** Yellowstone so that all people could enjoy it. In 1872, Yellowstone became the world's first national park. Today, there are over 350 national parks in the United States.

President Ulysses S. Grant signed the paper that made Yellowstone the first national park in the United States.

ELLOWSTONE NATIONAL PARK

NATIO
PA
SER

Department
of the Interio

President
Ulysses S. Grant

Wonders of Yellowstone

Yellowstone is famous for its **geysers** (GUY-zuhrz), hot **springs**, and bubbling mud pools. These form when heat, rocks, and water press against each other beneath Earth's **crust**. This causes cracks to form at the weak spots in Earth's surface. Hot mud, steam, and water escape through the cracks.

At Mammoth Hot Springs, hot water pushes up from inside Earth. The water flows over the soft rock and slowly changes the rock into different shapes.

Many kinds of tiny plants and animals grow in the warm water at Mammoth Hot Springs. This is what gives Mammoth Hot Springs its different colors.

What Is a Geyser?

Geysers are hot springs that erupt from below the ground and shoot hot water and steam into the air. There are more than 300 geysers in Yellowstone National Park. Many people come to Yellowstone just to see them.

The most famous geyser in Yellowstone is named Old Faithful. It erupts every half hour to two hours and can shoot a stream of water more than 150 feet into the air!

Visitors to the park can watch Old Faithful erupt, but they must stay about 300 feet away to be safe.

Buffalo

At one time, there were almost no buffalo left in the park because hunters had killed most of them. Now the rules of the park protect buffalo so people can't harm them.

Animal Life

Yellowstone is home to many animals. The park has more than 275 kinds of birds. Its rivers and lakes are full of many kinds of fish. There are also moose, elk, buffalo, wolves, deer, and bighorn sheep. Buffalo are the largest animals in the park. An adult buffalo can weigh up to 2,000 pounds and stand over six feet tall! Buffalo may look big and slow, but they can run faster than a person can.

Elk

Bighorn sheep

The Wolves of Yellowstone

In the early 1900s, people were afraid that the wolves in Yellowstone might harm people and kill too many animals. Some of the wolves were destroyed. Other wolves were trapped and taken away from Yellowstone to live somewhere else.

Some people believed that wolves were a natural part of animal life in the park. In 1995, wolves were brought back into Yellowstone. Now there are several families of gray wolves living in the park.

Gray wolves hunt elk for food. The wolves help to keep the Yellowstone elk herd from getting too large and eating the plants that other animals also need to live.

Forest Fire!

Most of Yellowstone is covered by grassy meadows and pine tree forests. If there is not enough rain, the grasses and trees get very dry and can catch fire easily.

There was not much rain in Yellowstone in 1988. **Lightning** started several big forest fires in the park. More than one-third of the forest was destroyed. More than 25,000 firefighters were needed to control the fire. Today, new trees, bushes, and grass are growing in the burned areas. Over time, the forest will return.

By carefully following the park rules, visitors can help protect the park from forest fires and other dangers.

Things to Know About Yellowstone

Every year, more than 2 million people from all over the world visit Yellowstone. The park has more than 350 miles of roads and 1,200 miles of trails. In the summer, visitors can go camping, hiking, fishing, and horseback riding. In the winter, visitors can go skiing and snowshoe hiking.

We can help protect Yellowstone by following the park's rules and leaving the land the way we found it. That way, Yellowstone will always be there for all of us to enjoy.

Glossary

canyon   A deep valley with high, steep sides.

crust   The top layer of Earth.

erupt   To burst out of something.

explore   To travel to new places to find new things.

geyser   A spring under the ground that sometimes shoots hot water and steam into the air.

glacier   A large body of ice that moves slowly across a wide area of land.

lightning   A flash of light caused by electricity passing between a cloud and Earth.

pioneer   A person who is one of the first to go to a new place.

protect   To guard something against harm.

spring   A place where water under the ground bubbles to the surface.

trapper   Someone who uses things like cages and nets to catch animals.

volcano   An opening in Earth's surface through which hot liquid rock is sometimes forced.

Index